Prayers to the Universe

Poems
by

Julie Excell

WalkerDoodle Press

Copyright © 2019 Julie Excell
All rights reserved.

No part of this book may be reproduced or transmitted in any form or by any means, electronic or mechanical, including photocopying, recording, or by any information storage and retrieval system without the expressed written permission of the author, except in the case of brief quotations in critical articles and reviews.

ISBN- 978-0-9984554-7-1

Cover design by Ling Sigstedt

WalkerDoodle Press
Denver, CO 80220

This book is dedicated to Art Elser and the JUC poetry group, without whom it would not exist.

Contents

Hodgepodge Universe 1
All I Can Do 2
What Are We Waiting For? 3
Upon Seeing Henry Tanner's Painting of the Annunciation 4
Coming Soon 5
A Walk Through My Tourist Town 6
On the Bus to Las Vegas 8
Love Letter to the Rockies 10
Autumn Song 11
Fall 12
Winter Again: Holding On 13
Cat, Summer, Patio 14
Concatenation 15
Sonnet for ZuZu 16
Anima Dreams 17
Puzzle Pieces 18
Exploring Desire 19
At the End of Our Fling 20
Boundaries 22
Lexophilia 23
Cooking: Me, You 24
Fight With Me 25
Divorce Spring 26
Fuck 27

Obfuscating the Definition of Subterfuge	28
For Jane	29
Cooking With Crystal and Victoria	30
Taking Flight	32
Plaiting Janie's Hair	33
After the Workshop With the Poet Laureate	34
A Photo of Us in Muir Woods	35
Minus Tide	36
Between Here and Gone	37
Learning to Fly	38
Kindling Sticks	39
Through the Wall	40
Spring Again: Tulip Waits	41
Writer's Block	42
On the Stairs	43
Sonnet to My Heart	44
Prayer to the Universe	45
About the Author	46

Hodgepodge Universe

My scientist friend tells me,
leaning back and sipping beer,
that dandelions pretend to have sex.
They put on a show, he says,
but in fact they're all clones.

I try to take this in.
Why, I ask, leaning forward,
Why is it like that?

Evolution, he shrugs, smiling,
is messy, it leaves things behind.
It keeps its options open, and moves on;
it's all about how to survive,
not the most efficient design.

Here is my prayer:

Thank you, force behind the Bang,
for this hodgepodge universe
built of a reckless drive,
a quark-deep need
to unfold and keep unfolding,
any damn way we can.

Thank you,
from the center of my messy heart
for your poetry-seeding,
star-wheeling
mystery.

All I Can Do

In the church of the holy question
I sit next to a woman with a visitor's badge
and afterward I ask her about herself.
Five minutes later she's crying,
scrubbing away the tears so hard
I'm afraid she'll break the skin.

It's hard to come here without my husband, she says,
I picture him next to me on the bench.
How long has it been, I ask, and she answers
twenty-seven months; but how can I go on,
when he was my life? I prayed for him,
and he came, but why did he have to leave?
I'm sorry, she tries to smile,
I'm sorry — I don't tell people this,
but somehow I felt you'd understand.

Please, I say, please don't apologize,
please accept my thanks.

It's no good wondering if I can write,
after you said you'd love me half as much
without my poems. No good wondering
what it is I need to say, or if it will clang
false when I read it to you.
No good wondering if I can love
like she can, knowing what there is to lose.
All I can do is show up
every morning in the stained-glass light of dawn
with my open pad and pen. All I can do
is listen in the silence on the stairs,
and hold onto the fact that she's right —
I understand.

What Are We Waiting For?

God it's hard to think, with everything waiting.
The handle of my cup arching for my hand,
the newspaper gagged in its bag,
my cat's back twitching,
the fruit vamping in the bowl,
pipes pounding against the taps,
shoes unbearably empty on the mat,
keys on the hook yearning
for their locks, glass
made to be looked through,
the door designed
to be opened, and
you alone
in your space,
me
in mine.

Upon Seeing Henry Tanner's Painting of the Annunciation

Mary sits on a plain, rumpled bed in a bare chamber.
She is not dressed as an Empress or as a nun,
but as what she was: an ordinary Jewish woman,
wearing a simple brown shift, unadorned.
Her hands are folded, in submission, or in fatigue.
Her head is slightly lowered as she looks calmly up at the vision
before her — the vision that tells her she will bear God within her.
And what does she see? — not an angel, no rush of wings,
only a bright and steady light. Only a shaft of light.
Her face speaks of patient awareness, contemplation, acceptance.

Before he passed from this world, the Buddha said
to those gathered around him, "Make of yourself a light."
Jesus said, "I am the light of the world.
Whoever follows me will never walk in darkness."
Audre Lorde said, "For women, poetry is not a luxury.
It forms the quality of the light within which we predicate
our hopes and dreams toward survival and change,
first made into language, then into idea, then into action."

Mary sits calmly on a rumpled bed,
dressed in a plain brown robe, her feet bare.
Her calloused hands are folded, her face tilted
slightly up as she contemplates the vision before her:
a light, a bright shaft of light, simply a light.
And what is she thinking as she receives the message
that she will be the bearer of light

Coming Soon

Walking from church to home
I pass a white-haired woman
with a wooden cartful of artifacts,
leather straps, baskets, ancient
wheels and poles the same as in
Constantinople or Pompeii
before the fall.

She's wearing a turban hat
with tassel, white knit gloves
with brown palms,
and she points ahead as
she passes and says,
"It's coming soon, I guess."

I have just time
to glance around, to nod,
"I guess so"
before she's gone.

Did she mean the light,
changing to Walk?
Did she mean the bus coming
for to carry, did she mean
the snow forecast for today and
rolling in like ash,
did she mean evening,
did she mean
the end,
did she mean
change?

A Walk Through My Tourist Town

Last night I walked through downtown:
A woman trying to sell her jewelry
from the trunk of her car. Two men
playing spangled accordions, a group of five
big boys with backpacks following their leader
Where we goin' Dan? Hey Dan!
What does this Dan have I wonder but they're gone.
A thin girl standing on a wall in soft leather boots
and a dress made of colored scarves
playing a wooden flute, or at least
seeming to play I can't hear at all
through the throng.
Panhandlers among us I avoid their eyes
like everyone else.
One sits, head in hands, old with a wooden bowl
containing three nickels and a dime.
I put a dollar in and
he looks up, startled. We nod.
I'm sorry life is so hard.
Life's so goddamn hard sometimes.

Across the block on the non-tourist side,
a man stands in a doorway, playing the saxophone,
his eyes closed, no hat out for tips.
I stop and listen, leaning
on a post. A couple materializes
with a baby — a baby all light
with soft hair standing up
like a cat's, a cocky, tiny face
all smiles, white arm waving,

watching the man with the
shiny horn. We stand and slowly
the sax man opens his eyes.
      Joy all around.
For a moment in the twilight
free simple plain old joy
all around.

On the Bus to Las Vegas

As we pass through these mountains on our way to Vegas,
I'm afraid we are temporarily beyond the reach of internet
or cell phone service. We ask you not to panic. To help you
remain calm, we will offer some antiquated diversions.
Next to you, there is a window through which you may look
to observe the outside world. As you may or may not be aware,
it is currently spring. For your diversion, we have researched
some facts about spring, which is the transition season between winter
and summer (of course it is always summer in Vegas!)
This transition has some quaint and mildly diverting results.
First, there is the return of color to the winter world.
It is a little known fact that there are more colors to spring
than just the traditional green. I direct your attention to the branches
of the bushes next to the creek. You may notice that they are bright
orange, shading to chartreuse at the tips, where the new leaves will
    burst.
The plum trees near them have leaves of deep wine red, not unlike
the velvet curtains at the King Casino! The willow shoots are yellow,
and hung with soft seed pods, which appear almost as plush as the
    carpet
you will find on the casino floor! Next we will pass through a stand
of pear trees in full bloom. The white petals are falling-- if the
    windows
opened, you could perhaps feel them brush your arm, and if we were
to stop, you could perhaps kick through the white drifts which have
    formed,
and which rush, full of fragrance I am told, on the breeze nearly as
    cool
as your air-conditioned, luxurious hotel rooms. You could also
    perhaps
look up, as I am told the spring sky is bright and soft, deep and
    changing,
though surely not as bright as the flashing lights on the slot machines!

But please do not concern yourselves — the bus is hermetically sealed, and we will not stop until we reach the covered parking structure, where all danger of exposure has been eliminated. Now enjoy the film!

Love Letter to the Rockies

Getting me through this asphalt-gray day:
a vision of the Rocky Mountains in spring,
where last night in my dream
I ran off the road
into the birth of river from snow.

And then all was quiet and we were alone,
me and the mountains, blue-gray and shining,
jagged wet stone soaring up canyon walls,
turning to orange and rose.

Thin air, thin creek, made of nothing
but H, 2, and O, or maybe,
this high up,
one and a half at most.

Yet somehow from the inch of soil at the canyon top,
a congregation of pines,
Indian paintbrush still wet,
chokecherry bushes snapping spicy
in the shafts of purest sun.

I don't know how the roots
can run so deep,
but they do.

Autumn Song

The plum tree strews the path
with her bright brave fruit,
like the Mexican woman at the street fair,
her weavings radiating a thousand miles of sun.
The plump globes pop beneath my boot
as I hurry nowhere, somewhere, pursued
by whirling leaves, the last reckless roses,
a rattling battalion of seeds, a flurry
of bright notes falling through the air:
the time has come, they shout,
to bare your crimson heart, to fling out
your gold, to spread the harvest of your soul,
across the bright blanket, in the last rays
of precious, piercing light.

Fall

It's more than just the slanting light,
calling through the yellow leaves,
more than bright falling to bright, more
than rustling whispers rushing
you down the street. Things
are on the move, loose, poised,
sunflower galaxies spin, shedding
petals of stardust, supernova roses burst,
cosmic clouds of seed fluff whirl,
ready to transform, to enter the flow.
How we yearn to fall,
to dissolve, to trust that we will rise,
changed, how we long
to let go.

Winter Again: Holding On

thank god for that crow
I just heard claiming it's dawn,
and behind me the click
of my cat's yawn, and
the eight-minute return
of my daughter's snooze alarm,

because last night winter came so hard
it cut off the kamikaze cry of the last pansy,
and stole the green hum of the lawn,
the rattle of seed pods, the cottonwood's
applause.

and now I have to rattle the spoons,
bang the pans like drums,
beat the eggs loud in a tin bowl;
I want to call someone
and fight on the phone,
because I need to hear it:
Hey! I'm still alive here,
still holding on.

Cat, Summer, Patio

She loves the warm breeze,
loves the way it shakes the leaves
and ruffles grasses, chasing white
butterflies up from the clover.

She lounges under the wrought-iron chair,
green eyes half-closed, ears alive,
pink bundle of nose lifted,
sleek sides pulsing fast in and out
(she is not concerned so much
with breathing as with taking in
the greatest wealth of smells.)

She looks up at me and blinks,
isn't everything
simply perfect
right now?

Concatenation

The contumacious Pomeranian
escaped its confines, comingled
with a conniving labradoodle,
and descended upon a complex of cats
sunning circumspect on the sandstone.
Consequently, a rare conjunction of feline
ferocity converged to create the declaration
of a new puss-state, a united concentration—
a powerful CONCATENATION!
Meee-yow!!

Sonnet for ZuZu

So what is there to love about my cat,
when plainly she regards me as her fool,
A puzzling butler clumsy in her path
and slow to scratch her back or fill her bowl?
Nor will my cat return my love in kind —
she will not run to greet me when I call
her name, or fear to snub me if she finds
my ministrations less than bountiful.
Yet when she lets me pet her whipped-cream chest,
or rub her tiny felt and velvet head,
it's like I'd coaxed a wild bird to rest
upon my palm and make my hand its bed.
To love a thing so beautiful and proud
is privilege that is its own reward.

Anima Dreams

How long can I go on
loving your twin brother
being starved in your attic?
No human eye has ever seen him,
just a flame at night
at the top of the house,
through the shutters,
the sound of tap-dancing.

Face to face, I imagine him pale
and droll and laughing until he cries,
dressed in drag
from your grandmother's dusty trunk,
weaving tapestries from your old ties.
Leaping up when he sees me,
grabbing my hands and gushing,
"We must have tea and talk!"
and telling me all
your secret
feelings.

So, I wait
in the dust on the stair,
And he'd better be there, bud,
he'd better be there.

Puzzle Pieces

Dump your thousand-piece puzzle next to mine
on the dim wooden table damp from the barmaid's towel,
and we'll let our partly assembled sections rub and tumble,
each revealing a piece of the bigger scene:
A carefully chosen shirt, a favorite shoe, a lined eye,
deliberate stubble, self-conscious mole, biceps from the gym,
painted hair, squint lines, practiced smiles.

The overall picture is not yet clear, but your tabs want
to fit in my slots, my curves yearn for your points,
Let's rattle it all into one box and take it somewhere,
Let's slide our pieces around, let's see what fits,
The puzzle longs for completion, holes to be filled,
the Mystery to emerge.

Exploring Desire

The dictionary says
it comes from the French, *desirer*,
going back to the Latin, "to long for."
But even this goes back to *de sidere*,
which means "from the stars."

But since the stars are far away,
and this book has slid to the floor,
and since *sidere* means "heavenly body,"
perhaps you
could help me
explore.

At the End of Our Fling

Can I keep the gifts?
I don't mean the frozen leftover ravioli,
the blues CD that predicted our end,
or the half-bottle of capers mysterious
in the fridge, and you can have back
the films we never managed to finish
before waltzing upstairs.

And I'll send you back the book
you loaned me that I'm halfway through
(though I'll miss the passion of your scrawls
in the margins and the places you underlined
right through the words, freeing me
to write them myself).

What I mean is the permissions I have given
myself since you came along: that I may
toss the gray fruit bowl from my mom
that cast its pall on my apples for years
and replace it with an extravagant one from Mexico,
and that I may wear unnecessary and
impractical underwear, or none at all;

And the visas granted for free passage
from heart to head, border barricades down,
prisoners exchanged or set free,
censorship lifted of certain words
related to what I want and what I fear.

And most of all, the flow of poems
and the knowing in my bones
that these things come
from me, not you,
and not even from me but
from somewhere deeper,
somewhere love never ends.

Boundaries

Something there is that loves and hates a wall.
That day at the coast we ran in the waves,
over the border where ocean meets land, meandering the sand
until the sun crossed the line between sea and sky, flashing green
as day met night, you took my hand.
Something there is in me that aches to let you in,
something there is that holds you apart;
I turned and picked up the shell of a crab,
you brushed the sand from your skin,
we turned to go inside, you measuring me with your eyes,
holding the door, then letting it slam.

Lexophilia

On our first date, lovers as we were of words,
he gave me *cacography*, with a story about his ex,
who never accepted his note of apology,
because his handwriting was like a house falling down.

I came back with *revenant*, and we savored it,
a friend one had thought dead, returning,
with the sound of a stalled car starting on a wintry road.

And in spite of the risks of accepting expensive gifts,
I couldn't say no when he murmured in my ear, *houghmagandy*
a word forbidden from my dictionary, between *hot tub* and *hound*
with its onomatopoeia dance-of-love sound.

Later, he breathed through my hair, like the moon through clouds,
a luscious word starting with L that I couldn't hear
through the flabbergast, the concupiscence, the yen.

I searched for it later, when I was alone—
somewhere between *levitation* and *lightning*,
but surely, I told myself, nowhere near *love*.

Cooking: Me, You

You make us all sweat:
purple eggplant splayed
and rubbed down with coarse salt,
the chicken swooning in its pot, so close
but not quite coming
to a boil, and me, watching you.

Sitting on a corner of the countertop,
swinging my legs and wishing you'd
step between them and pull me close,
but you're bending over the recipe book,
tracing the sacred text with fingertips,
moving your lips, setting me to mincing
and simmering, muttering magical words:
caper, julienne, reduce, braise.

Oh braise me brazen, love,
sear my heart and lay it open
in the miracle of this love poem
you've made of my sterile home,
infuse me through with spice
and simmer me where it's hot and slow,
till I'm tender and falling
off my bones.

Fight With Me

Fight with me
close and hard
against the foyer wall, cracking
the mirror, flattening the boots,
at the kitchen table, knocking
cups and peels aside,
splitting the cutting board.

Take me on anytime,
three AM, quarter to nine,
at twilight cutting
through the yard,
catch me on the bench and
set me screaming at the stars,
hit me with your best stuff, and
settle for nothing but mine.

As long as later
oh my love
we get past words
to what we know
with breath and hands
and hearts
and eyes.

Divorce Spring

here's a (tremblingly
        in my hand rain slapping)

letter
   (love means everynothing while the
        hills battle clouds greenwhitegreen)

a letter saying (sunshadow
        across the page
              falling)
our divorce is final
   (love is every-
              thingnothing all
      the earth then
      a print on the track)

& suddenly i'm rootlessgrowing

      whole,
           half

Fuck

and now accepting the prize
for Most Satisfying Word
let's hear it for
fuck.

for those having trouble
saying it, just catch your lip
with your teeth and blow
until you can't hold it anymore: *fff*--
then open your mouth and let go
in a groan: *uuh*, catching your breath
at the back of your throat
until it breaks through with a crash, *kuh*,
as in kiss as in crazy
as in catastrophe, chaos, close, come.

of course it's easier to say it right
than to do it right,
which involves something deeper
than just breath and body parts,
and best of luck finding someone
to help you
with that.

Obfuscating the Definition of Subterfuge

It's a word you murmur, at twilight,
out of breath at the end of an alley, in the rain,
at an iron gate swinging open with a keen
onto an empty space where something
important was supposed to stand.

It's a word that whispers something underground,
a hidden munitions dump, a cavern-lab
where scarred scientists take senseless risks
for a cause no one can explain.

Subterfuge. Subterfugial force,
spinning us away from the truth, sub-
terranean fugitive, strange suburban machine,
it's a mystery deep as *hypotenuse*,
ssshh--don't ask me
what it means!

For Jane

The spring she was five
she came versing in
from the green (she was born
knowing what poetry is):
    Mama it's a prantillic vouquet
    of chanting smellarams!
And I grokked her joy
and breathed it in.

One of ahundredish
lessons from her: Let go
of your pompish need
to make sense,
and your borious slavence
to the words Webster
pinsected to the page--
Let go and let the music in.

And now she's leaving
to try on lives, and I can't
sing can't hum can't even
breathe how much
I'll miss the
prantillic
vouquet of her.

Cooking With Crystal and Victoria

I'm cooking with my daughter —
she is eight years old.
We're on our own TV Cooking Show —
"Cooking With Crystal and Victoria."
(We choose different names each time).
The TV camera is in the microwave
over the stove.

She says, "Welcome back
to Cooking With Crystal and, um,
Victoria! Victoria, I mean, Crystal,
what are we doing now?"
And I say, "Well, Crystal,
I mean, Victoria,
now the noodles are done
and we're going to take them out
and put them in the pan we have prepared
for our world-famous lasagna!"

And she holds up the pan,
striking several poses
so the audience can see it from every side.
And she asks, smiling for the camera,
"And then do we put on
the Cheesy Mixture, Victoria?"
And I say, "Well, actually, Crystal,
we put on the sauce first."
Then she says, very seriously,
holding up the bottle of sauce,
"Now remember, folks,
we use *only* — and she looks at the label
— *only* Mushroom Supreme!"

Then I'm taking the noodles
out of the hot water, and they're
slipping, and I'm burning myself,
and we're laughing and she's saying,
"Heh. heh! Now remember folks,
don't do what Crystal is doing!"
And I'm singing, "Yes, folks,
Ouch, ouch Crystal is burning herself
— maybe we'd better go to a commercial!"

And we're laughing
and I'm running cold water
over my hand and she's saying
wouldn't it be cool if they really
had a show like that
— with real people
doing real things and
making mistakes and being funny?

And I can smell the tomato sauce
and the garlic and see
the smear of ricotta
on her cheek, and it is warm
and steamy in the kitchen
and snowing outside
and I love her so much
I love her so
much I love her
so
much

Taking Flight

They're digging down
the playground
where you stood
on the highest rung
my fear allowed you,
and called to the crows
in the tops of the cottonwoods
across the park.

And you believed
they answered you,
believed they understood you,
you believed so beautiful,
while I stood underneath,
craning up at you,
my arms outstretched,
as if in supplication.

Oh suspend me,
for just one call —
lift me up,
let me just once
think not of falling,
but of taking flight.

Plaiting Janie's Hair

I plait Janie's hair
in the quiet of early morning,
in a patch of passing sun,
before the bathroom mirror.

Her book is propped on the sink,
she is lost in it, far away,
leaning heedless against my heart.
My hand brushes her cheek, her ear,
moving through the garden of her hair,
I close my eyes and breathe
its wild marigold musk.

I braid slowly, shyly,
thrilled by the smell and feel of her,
by this chance to stroke
her wild and dappled head,
before she bolts,
and is gone.

After the Workshop With the Poet Laureate

Dipping each fry delicately in red,
you gazed out the window behind me,
then you said, "Wouldn't it be great
if that was a painting of a window,
and not just glass?"
And I shrugged, not bothering to turn,
"Why not just have the window then? "

And you stared at me, your mother
who for years had hoarded her poems,
and who hadn't heard a word the man had said.
"Because if someone painted it,
it would make people really *see* it."
I turned my silly stiff neck, and you pointed,
"See? How that red car colors the white?
And that orange sign reflected in the puddle,
and that spark — do you see that blue spark
in the headlight there?"

And I did see it, then — the curving shadow of the stairwell
against the silo behind, the gleaming leaves,
the stunning clouds every shade
but white, and I saw the spark,
that incandescent spark that you are —
that you are,
thank you.

A Photo of Us in Muir Woods

My daughter, seated on a shadowed bench,
leans her head against my waist as I stand next to her,
my hair aflame with late sunlight breaking
through the branches of the redwoods.

The tree behind us looms huge as a fairytale tower,
dark, ridged, rising from the core of the earth,
reaching almost to the sun, a silent monolith,
still as stone, but living, a presence, an ancient force

considering us, our lives a half-second of its age,
rootless, flickering, our bodies of nothing but dust. Still,
perhaps the moment when I cradled her head and
we looked together down the long columns of shadow and light,
aware for a heartbeat of the true size of things,
made a tiny, lovely wave in one of its thousand rings.

Minus Tide

The day the cosmos heaved the ocean back
past all lines it had drawn,
I stepped from bristling rock to rock,
that yesterday were undersea, or islands
rough and remote as the moon.

The cliff I clutched for balance
wasn't rock at all,
but a shuttered city of ivory
barnacles and indigo mussels
steep-roofed and shining.

I leaned an hour over a pool:
weeds revealed as whiskered anemones,
black pyramids of shell that suddenly
thrust out a foot and danced,
a golden stone that became a Buddha-crab,
its claws laid before it on the sand.

You're gone, too,
and this gift of a world
that you've left me
will soon be covered again,
though I'll never stop probing
its tough and splendid life.

Between Here and Gone

In the garage, in the place between
home and gone, my daughter
sulks sullen in the dusk
of the backseat, testing me again.

I am looking back at thirteen,
remembering my own sonar bursts
of sharp, wild words,
sent out to map the landscape,
to find what stayed solid enough
for me to crash against.

My love for her settles around us,
essential and scarred as this old car,
sighing into silence, into prayer:
give me strength to hold steady,
to be ready to start again, full.

Learning to Fly

I will be captain of my spaceship,
though it has been a tinker toy craft,
and though it's true I've caused it to crash
a million times, and had to rebuild,
unskilled, and with outlandish tools:
pencil, hills, a lever of morning light.

I will be captain of my spacecraft,
though I have given over the seat in the past,
to others who tied a line to the com,
and jacked it along in the wake of their path.

I have cut those ties and floundered adrift,
sideways, woblonged, nose-dived, daft.
But I will be captain of my spacecraft,
even if my mission is just
to learn to fly, at last.

Kindling Sticks

In the gray of winter I make a list
of things to use as kindling sticks, as
wedges to open cracks for light,
as brushes to spread the light like paint,
as prayers to keep my faith alive.

At the top of it is the mesa trail
through the congregation of pines,
the carpet of larkspur and kinnikinic,
the climax of rock with the endless view,
the valley where wind rolls the grass like waves.

Next is my Irish friend Kathleen,
who lives at the coast, and in my heart,
who always sees the best in me, giving me
the grace to make it so.

On my best days I add
my mistakes to the list,
for how they've (haven't they?)
helped me grow.

May I make it so.

Through the Wall

I remember presenting my poems to Maya Emerson
in our college dorm. She was older and wore herself
with bohemian ease, she was a writer, she would warn you
straight out, not *trying to be*, or *planning*, but *was*.

I had written a weighty mass, mostly long and thin,
with images that mumbled and buzzed, rising
at times to an almost comprehensible quack,
like your parents' party heard through the bedroom wall,
when you're seven and can't sleep, kicking off the sheets,
snuffling their mysterious smoke and brew and
wondering in the dark, clutching your bear,
at your mother's wild laugh
like nothing heard on earth before.

I waited forever for her praise, then one day
found them shoved, unmarked, under my door.
Her silence about them swelled under my skin
until it exploded, blowing open my eyes.
My poems were bad.
The horizon jammed sideways, my teddy bear swore,
dogs sneered, my desk was sinister, and trees,
all my clothes were jokes, I discovered
I was deaf in one ear and dumb in the other,
ashamed of my very soul.

But I kept writing. Covering it, like Austen,
when someone came through the door. I needed
to press my ear to the wall, to whack at the plaster —
I could almost hear it, almost get it down,
the sound of the Universe, that wild laugh,
those secret words never heard before.

Spring Again: Tulip Waits

The rest of the tulips
in the vase stand straight,
but one, I see suddenly,
glancing up from the page,
has bent forward to fix me
in its spotlight gaze.

How can I read?
I slide my book aside
and stare back as clocks tick
and snow slips *whump*
from the courtyard trees.
A bird tries some notes.
Time passes, everything breathes.

At its center are six stamen
shaped like microphones:
Lean in, it whispers:
Say it now-- say it!
What you were born to say —
there's no more time to waste.

Writer's Block

Winter has come to worry
my little head and suddenly
empty hands like the limbs
of the Japanese maple outside my door,
gone from green to valentine red
to vacant gray.

The forecast is for patches
of freezing fog on the stairs,
spreading to the desk, where
it will cloud the consonant keys,
stealing the galloping fun
of *w*, the railroad clatter
of *t* and *k*, the luscious melting
of *l* and *m*, sensuous *s*
and mysterious *x* and *v*

leaving me with nothing
but a sigh, a whine —
oh, ah, ee,
no u, only cold
little i.

On the Stairs

My friend says it's hilarious
that I sit before dawn
halfway down the stairs
with my pad and pen.

Hilarious. Which part?
The stairs I guess,
but here's what he doesn't know:

It's the only place that's not papers,
not lists, containers, minute hands.
It's not please, avoid, regret,
it's not when, why, how;
It's the only place still
and now.

The light grows through the window
at the bottom of the stairs, steel gray to rose.
It shows me the truth of the marigolds,
the empty iron chair, the paper
on the step, a passing cat, a crow.

It's an act of faith, waiting there.
A miracle when words appear,
out of no words, on the page.
And can't words change the morning?
Can't words change the world?

Sonnet to My Heart

Inside me beats my brave Cassandra heart,
my heart that knows no less than everything.
Night after night it pulls my lies apart,
Day after day I'm deaf to what it sings.
My eyes, my ears, my nose, my fingertips
always so busy bringing me the news,
my slick Narcissus brain its mirror grips,
my heart flies wild and sings its lonely blues.
It sends me notes in dreams, in songs, in poems,
it whispers truths between my empty words,
it urges me to bring my soul back home,
to break my rigid shell in silly shards.
Cassandra let me hear you, let me know,
let me have faith, beloved, help me grow.

Prayer to the Universe

Dear ever-Expanding,
      show me how to expand,
Dear Ever-Unfolding,
      teach me to unfold
Dear Recklessly Rushing to Reach Higher,
      help me to raise my arms,
      if I am made of stardust, then
      use me as your avatar:
Blow me open, spin me around,
Burn me bright in this man-made mire,
on this lost and lovely blue-green ball,
oh claim me, claim me
and make me whole.

About the Author

Julie started writing poetry when she was about twelve years old. She has since gone on to write plays, and other works. Her greatest inspirations have been her daughter Jane, and the general mystery of the Universe.

www.ingramcontent.com/pod-product-compliance
Lightning Source LLC
Chambersburg PA
CBHW020431010526
44118CB00010B/532